A

SERMON

UPON

THE SUBJECT OF DEITY,

PREACHED ON SUNDAY, SEPT. 9,

BY

RICHARD CARLILE,

FROM THE PULPIT, BEFORE THE CONGREGATION,

OF

THE CHURCH

OF

MOUNT BRINKSWAY,

NEAR STOCKPORT,

FORMERLY, BEFORE THEIR CONVERSION, THE CONGREGATION

OF

BIBLE CHRISTIANS,

AND

PRINTED AT THEIR REQUEST.

London:

PRINTED AND PUBLISHED BY R. CARLILE, 62, FLEET
STREET.

1827.

Price Sixpence.

A

SERMON,

&c.

To whom then will ye liken God? or what likeness will ye compare unto him?—ISAIAH, chap. xl. ver. 18.

THE subject intended for this morning's Discourse is that of Deity. It is a subject of the highest importance, in relation to the present understandings of mankind. It is that which agitates all men, about which, for the want of more understanding, they disagree—but a weighty matter on which there should not be the least disagreement. The time, I trust, will come, when there shall be no disagreement on this important consideration, and when, to use the language of allegorical inspiration, " *the knowledge of the Lord shall cover the earth, as the waters cover the sea.*"

Much has been said about Deists and Atheists; great outcry and condemnation has been heard about Deism, Atheism, and Materialism; but few seem to understand the subject. In relation to the physical powers of the universe, or in relation to whatever we know of those powers, THERE CAN BE NEITHER DEISTS NOR ATHEISTS. I know no such man as an *Atheist*, in that acceptation which makes the word relate to the physical powers of the universe. I know nothing of *Atheism*, but in relation to the contemptible idols of very superstitious people; and here all rational beings are alike Atheists. I am an Atheist toward the superstitious man, who makes his God, or idol, and gives him attributes which I cannot see, and, consequently, to the existence of which I cannot consent; but I am not an Atheist in relation to any rational or respectable view of Deity, to any thing that is *known* of Deity by mankind. I deny not GOD in the larger sense of the word; but what I do deny is, the propriety of a man's so figuring the Deity by his imagination, as to reduce it to the standard of a being like himself, and to endow it with his own trifling attributes.

The terms Deism and Atheism, then, have no relation to the physical powers of the universe; but they relate only to those imaginations and false pictures which mankind have, from time to time, raised up about those powers. They form a mere dispute about words, and not about any thing known to be in existence; therefore, the more sensible man will neither boast of being either Atheist or Deist. They are idle words, words of dispute, that have no meaning, and about which wise men will not dispute. Let the disputants ask each other, or themselves, what they mean by the words of what they know, and they will find that alike they know nothing.

Through all the records which we have of mankind, we find them either inquisitive, or superstitiously and ignorantly positive upon the subject of Deity.

The Hindoos, of whom we have the earliest records, have reduced their imaginations of the power of Deity to a variety of figures. Of the allegories of those figures we are entirely ignorant, and that ignorance, as far as we know, extends even to the modern Hindoos.

The Persians held and have retained a sublimity of idea in relation to the Deity, which equals, if it do not exceed, that of any other people; and to that sublimity of idea we owe every thing in the Bible that approaches to it; to that the language of my text is due—" *To whom then will ye liken God; or what likeness will ye compare unto him.*"

The elegant mythology of the Greeks and Romans has sprung from the imagination of figures for the various known physical powers of matter in the universe, and for all the passions of mankind. As devout before the statues of their Deities, as ever was Christian before the shrine of his favourite saint, they felt not, imagined not, that the power of the Deity resided and presided in the figure; but that the figure was a piece of human art to encourage the contemplation of a power that existed in a larger sense, or every where. There was nothing outrageous to human feeling or to good sense in the Pagan mythology. The notions of Deity held by the Greek and Roman philosophers were those which are held by the wisest men of the present day. They were inquisitive, and not positive. They felt as wise men will always feel, that they knew nothing on the subject for a certainty, and that they have every thing to learn. Let us but know this, and there will be no Atheists among us. We shall then come to a standard for uniformity of opinion.

More ignorant people, the Jews for instance, have had such degraded notions of Deity, as to reduce it to the figure of a man possessing all their varied passions. Not that I deny that this book, the Bible, has in some parts very sublime notions of the Deity; but those parts all appear to be of Persian extraction.

Among all the various views of Deity, I know of none that equals, in wisdom and sublimity, that view which is taken by the scientific Materialist. Without admitting any particular attribute, the Materialist denies none; and while contemplating the phenomena that surround him, he frankly acknowledges his entire ignorance of that incomprehensibility, which, while others pronounce incomprehensible, they have the vanity, inconsistency, and wickedness to attempt to define in attributes, while some are rash enough to proceed to being, figure, and location.

Much cry is made, much misconceived horror is expressed, at what is called Atheism, or Materialism. I have already stated my view of the word *Atheism*, I will now attempt to define to you what I understand by the word *Materialism*.

Materialism is the sum of human knowledge, in relation to physics. It has no pretensions beyond that knowledge. It may be termed universal chemistry, or the chemistry of animals, vegetables, minerals, and gases: the science of composition and decomposition. It embraces all mankind, every man is a Materialist, and if none had higher pretensions, insane pretensions, if all would confine themselves to the real amount of their knowledge, all would agree, and Materialism be the standard of their union. Materialism no where extendeth itself beyond the knowledge of man in wild speculation. It is every where and at all times *physical;* no where and at no time *metaphysical.* It is the wisdom of the wise man, and the folly of fools cannot resist it. It is that Deity, in " the elegant mythology of the Greeks," which represented the PRINCIPLE OF REASON, the sum of human knowledge, past, present, and to come.

The beauty of Materialism is at once seen in the humility and in the importance of its pretensions. Embracing every thing cognizable to the human senses, and consequently all-important, it has not one pretension that can be disputed. It suits itself alike to the modesty of the modest man—the meekness of the meek man—and the aspiring boldness of the bold and honest man. It removes timidity when understood, and, by its being a standard of criticism, lessens the conceit and arrogance of the false and assuming pretender to knowledge.

While I, a Materialist, will not allow that any man has a greater knowledge of Deity than myself, while I will not allow that any man has more real admiration and veneration of that power which we call Supreme, Deity, First Cause, God, or by whatever other name it passes among mankind—I cannot be so arrogant as to associate with my idea of that power any attribute that I find in myself. Criticism has reduced me to that state of humility, that I cannot associate that highest principle which I find in myself (the principle of intelligence) with an attribute, or as an attribute of that supreme power. And this is not my arrogance, but my humility, that brings me to this state of mind. How can I, who feel that I am nothing, associate myself with an attribute of that power which is every thing? These are the views and sentiments of a Materialist upon Deity—and these, I presume, are less objectionable than any view or sentiment that any pretender to religion has taken or held upon the subject. We disagree and dispute only where we are alike ignorant, not where we have knowledge. As *Materialism*, or that which has been decried as *Atheism*, is nothing in the human character but that simplicity, that innocence, that honesty, which modestly confines a man to speak of that with positiveness which he really doth understand—and not to speak of that, but in the spirit of enquiry, which he doth not understand; so it follows, that this character is at once the most humble and the highest state of man, and that the view of Deity which this character takes is superior to and more sublime, more worthy of respect, than that view which is taken by a deluded imagination, by a figuring and superstitious being.

Talking with preachers of the Christian religion, upon the subject of Deity, and I have conversed with many both of the Established Church and its Dissenters on this subject, I can uniformly bring them to an acknowledgment, that we know nothing positively about it—that to human senses it is incomprehensible—and that looking at it in a physical point of view, we can learn nothing of its attributes. But amidst this, confession of mutual ignorance, they fly to their pretended Bible revelation, and make of the Deity, which they have before admitted to be incomprehensible, a system of attributes. Here they travel beyond their knowledge, and it is here only, upon this speculative ground, that we disagree with, and dissent from, them. Can the fault of that dissent be ours? Is it not theirs? Are we to be reproached, because we will not venture on this speculative and uncertain ground? Is our honesty to be called insolence, our simplicity arrogance, and our modesty presumption? Yet such is the case, and the only consolation we have is, that they, who so reproach us, are insane, or not honest, on that topic.

I have no objection to the term *God, Deity, Supreme Power, First Cause,* or any other general and undefined attribute, as a matter of convenience in description, or in speaking of an existence which is supposed, but not known; but I object, I make a stand, I am inquisitive and critical, the moment I see or hear an attempt to endow that existence with any one particular attribute.

One thing should be observed, that whatever be our disputes in words about the character of that existence, those disputes can neither change the reality of that existence, nor affect its relations toward ourselves as identities or individual human beings. There can be no sin in our ignorance, no sin in honest and simple doubt, no sin in that humility which will not seek to cover its ignorance with arrogant presumption. The sin must all lie on the other side; it is theirs, not ours; we can have nothing to fear on this head.

The sum, then, of Materialism, is, that men are all alike Materialists as far as they have knowledge. All their knowledge is a knowledge of Materialism. Materialism is the point on which they all agree, and at which, it would be well, if they could all stay; but there are those who have a passion for specnlation in their cogitations and imaginations, who exceed in the range of their ideas all the bounds of knowledge, and who wander in a self-created labyrinth of mysticism and fiction, until they lose the right use of their senses. We dissent from such persons, inasmuch as we do not think it wise and proper to follow them into such a labyrinth. We seek more sure ground on which to tread, and we wait until they weary themselves, discover their errors, and return to us. We will assist, as far as we can, to remove them from this maze of error; but we cannot admit the propriety of the rash insanity which has led them into it. Materialism is, then, in brief, the point, or principle, that embraces the whole of mental sanity.

There is a particular point connected with this subject, and with that of every kind of Reform, to which I would summon your strict attention. In all first attempts to reform public institutions, that class of people, who are opposed to all institutions from a mere profligacy of character, will attempt to associate themselves with those who seek particular changes on well-formed grounds, and from calm, moral, and philosophical considerations. They are alike identified under the common name of Reformers, and the general opponent endeavours to draw the conclusion, with some instances in proof, that the whole spirit of the desired Reform is profligate. Discrimination is not always in the character of opposition, and it is here, on this ground, that every cause of Reform lingers and suffers.

It is, then, a matter of high importance, that we do all in our power to do, to discourage the connection with us of all profligate pretenders to Reform. Drunkenness is the more peculiar vice, the besetting sin, of this country, and is a prominent characteristic among those profligates to whom I am drawing your attention. Let not the drunkard be seen among you. If you meet him, let that meeting be for his reproof, and not as a common association. Our principles admit of our attaining the highest state of moral character among mankind; and the fault is our own, if we do not so distinguish ourselves. We can make others respect us only by so distinguishing ourselves; and the principle is common to the individual as well as to associations, that good character cannot be destroyed by the hand of an assassin; but must, to be lost, be suicidal.

The drunkard, though an enemy to self rather than to others, is abominable to a moral man, and I exhort you to shun and discountenance the character. Other vices claim your discrimination and discountenance; and if you proceed earnestly in the pursuit of moral strength, they will be found easy of detection and rejection. I do not impute vice to any people in classes; I do not claim for the alleged Atheist or Materialist a freedom from vice; I do not impute it as a necessary association with any particular opinions; I am above all narrow-minded prejudices of this kind; I wish you all to be so; and I would exhort all mankind to abstain from vices and to be moral, as the best foundation for general happiness, welfare, and improvement; and I exhort you to be the more particular, inasmuch as you stand before the public as the assumed Reformers of others.

Whatever Reforms we attempt, unless we build

them with moral views upon moral grounds, they can never be useful to us, or to our posterity. All government, all institutions, to be good, must have a moral foundation. Morality is the principle that applies to the whole of human action, and is that alone which can work to their welfare. The happiness of individuals must be based on morality, and the happiness of a community upon the aggregate action of such individuals. Others may send you to religion for happiness: I can see nothing there but the happiness of insanity or delusion; and, therefore, I call you, with your eyes open and minds sane, to the enjoyment of that happiness, that conscientiousness of right and well-doing, which is only to be deduced from a sense of morality.

As this principle of morality requires the aid of useful knowledge, and as that knowledge is more easily acquired by a strict criticism of the words we use, it behoveth us so to examine our language, as to see that the words have a strict relation to the things which they are intended to represent. There is another moral advantage to be gained from this observation. All the disputes among mankind, more particularly those about theology, are disputes about words, and not about things. A strict criticism upon the words we use, and a right understanding of the relation of those words to things, would prevent all those disputes. For instance :—

Different words and ideas are associated in different minds upon the subject of Deity. Now what is the real difference? Not about any thing, any particular power or quality that is known of Deity. When we fairly question ourselves and each other, we all frankly confess, that Deity is incomprehensible, and that we know nothing about it. The sum total, then, of the difference must be, in the words we use, in the different words which different persons have used in making expressions about Deity.

If we were to take those words which are variously

used upon the subject of Deity, or if each person would take his own words, put them upon paper, sift and try them every way as to their worth and proof, criticise them fairly as to their powers of description and representation, in relation to things and their qualities—he would positively find, that they stood for nothing, were good for nothing but to create disputes, and that they were utterly worthless when tested by any knowledge that we have of Deity. They prove nothing.

Language is the sonorous sign, or picture, or representation of things. The hand may paint or figure a copy or sketch of a thing comprehensible to the eye, or to the imagination—but the tongue, or voice, can describe by the power of language the qualities of a thing which the pencil cannot describe, otherwise than in those marks which are the signs of language ; cannot describe in picture. Can the pencil describe any thing of Deity ? Can language proclaim its qualities ? The answer must be *no,* if it be honest. Then about what are our disputes in relation to Deity ? What, but that we do not properly use our words about it.

Let this important consideration teach us carefully to criticise our own words, and as carefully to criticise the words of others, that we may avoid those mischievous disputes about theology and other matters, which are too common among mankind. Let us seek mutual instruction by mild conversations, and discourage the mere clamour of words, which are often words of sound but not of sense. If mankind could see their common interest, they would meet each other in the spirit of mutual instruction, and sit down to mild examination of self and of each other ; instead of hunting after subjects for sectarianism and perpetual dispute. Happiness being the aim or highest attainment of human life, we should mutually assist each other in its possession.

If I occupy more of your time, by enlarging upon the subject of this Discourse, I am not sure that I can add to the force or clearness of what I have already stated ; but as a recapitulation may impress the subject more deeply on your minds, I will so far trespass as to make it, and reverse the order of the points discoursed.

First, then, I trust, that I have made you fully sensible of the importance of criticising the words you are in the habit of using or hearing used, and of acquiring a full comprehension of their meaning and application, as the signs or representatives of certain things. This is a most important point in our self-education, and should form the basis of all education. It should be the peculiar object of the schools. Without attending to this point, it is impossible that we can acquire a correct knowledge of any thing. By attending to it, we shall remove the various sources of dispute, sectarianism, and contention, that have hitherto existed among mankind. This criticism upon our words will have the double effect of correcting our ideas, and of chastening our language. Theologians have introduced a variety of words into our language, that, when examined critically, are found to have no meaning. These words are the source of our dispute with them, and of their disputes with each other. To criticise the words, to shew that they have no meaning, is ample refutation of all the confused and mysterious doctrines which are spun upon them. Then let us avoid contention by this precaution, and entitle ourselves to assume a superiority among the various sects which, in these days of religious controversy, constitute the community.

Secondly—Upon the point of morals, there is much to which we ought most strictly to attend. As a precision in language will impress those with whom we converse with a sense of our literary superiority, it behoveth us at the same time to endeavour to command their farther and full respect, by leaving them no ground on which they can find fault with our morals. Without the aid of good morals, we cannot command the respect of our neighbours. With that aid, we may defy the malice of our most bitter enemies, whether they be theological, political, or immoral. In vain will they reproach us with infidelity or Atheism, so long as we reflect that reproach upon them with correct moral conduct.

Morals are not only necessary to command the respect of our friends or our enemies; but they are essential to our health, comfort, and general happiness. It is by them alone that we can make our homes cheerful and happy. And as far as responsibility to self, to society, or to a Deity, be in question, moral conduct must be the safe and approving guide.

Lastly—Upon the first and general point of my Discourse, the subject of Deity, little remains to be said, little can be added. If it be made a first point in the study of physics, it can rank but as secondary in relation to morals. To know where and when to acknowledge our ignorance, is the very summit of wisdom, and to do it in relation to Deity is the summit of veneration, and a due acknowledgment of our humility, of our sense of slight self-importance, in relation to that vast and incomprehensible power.

Let man but contemplate himself, the short period of his existence upon earth—his little consequence upon that earth—the immensity of the body of the planet in comparison with himself—the inferiority of that earth in relation to the size of other planets—its being but one of a number unknown, a mere speck in space, and man an imperceptible atom on that speck—then, what becomes of his vanity and arrogance, in associating himself with Deity, in making a God like himself, in giving figure, attributes, and location to the Deity? Would he do this, if he were in the habit of criticising the words he uses, in speaking of Deity? Would he do this, if he were a mild, moral, inquisitive being?

In conclusion, let me repeat to you the advantages which are to be gained by a strict adherence to every principle of morality. It will lead you, so to conduct yourself before the persons who may surround you, as to disarm malice and to perpetuate friendship. You will be valued as persons of integrity, on whom every moral reliance may be placed. You will be selected by others as the arbiters of right and wrong; right conduct being always seen in, or studied by, you. Whatever may be the nature of laws, or of appointments to the administration of those laws, the moral man is ever the ultimate judge in society—to him all appeals are made, and by him the character of public conduct is decided. The moral man has more real influence in society than that of which he is aware. Others may be selected to fill offices; but he is always in office. To this external influence may be added the internal and domestic influence which he will produce on himself and family, in health, in cheerfulness, in prosperity and general comforts. Disorder is prevented by temperance and precaution. Health is promoted by cleanliness and cheerfulness. Prosperity is insured by industry and regular application to business. These are also the principles of morality, and all within the compass of every man. Let not a vice be encouraged or winked at among you. Set your faces stedfastly against the domestic vice of drunkenness. Let the drunkard be never met by you without reproof. Shew the world, that while you are professed searchers after and lovers of truth, you are also the practisers of every precept that has hitherto proceeded from it. The precepts of morality are the precepts of truth. Morality embraces all the truths that have been discovered, and will embrace all those that shall hereafter be discovered. Shun not the truth, wherever it may lead you—and be not alarmed by the use of words against you, that have no relation to truth. Be firm, be valiant, in this your noble and moral warfare.

THE END.

Just published, price Sixpence,

THE GOSPEL according to RICHARD CARLILE; shewing, the True Parentage, Birth, and Life, of our Allegorical Lord and Saviour, JESUS CHRIST.

www.ingramcontent.com/pod-product-compliance
Lightning Source LLC
Chambersburg PA
CBHW082059070426
42452CB00052B/2752